Pebble® Plus
Bilingüe/Bilingual

GENTE DE LAS FUERZAS ARMADAS DE EE.UU./PEOPLE OF THE U.S. ARMED FORCES

SOLDADOS
DEL EJÉRCITO DE EE.UU.

SOLDIERS
OF THE U.S. ARMY

por/by Lisa M. Bolt Simons

Editora consultora/Consulting Editor: Gail Saunders-Smith, PhD

Consultor de contenido/Content Consultant: John Grady
Director de Comunicationes/Director of Communications
Association of the United States Army

CAPSTONE PRESS
a capstone imprint

Pebble Plus is published by Capstone Press,
151 Good Counsel Drive, P.O. Box 669, Mankato, Minnesota 56002.
www.capstonepub.com

Books published by Capstone Press are manufactured with paper
containing at least 10 percent post-consumer waste.

Library of Congress Cataloging-in-Publication Data
Simons, Lisa M. B., 1969–
[Soldiers of the U.S. Army. Spanish & English]
Soldados del Ejército de EE. UU. / por Lisa M. Bolt Simons = Soldiers of the U.S. Army / by Lisa M. Bolt Simons.
    p. cm.—(Pebble Plus bilingüe. Gente de las fuerzas armadas de EE.UU. =
Pebble Plus bilingual. People of the armed forces)
  Includes index.
  Summary: "A brief introduction to a soldier's life in the Army, including training, jobs, and life after service—in both
English and Spanish"—Provided by publisher.
  ISBN 978-1-4296-6118-8 (library binding)
  1. United States. Army—Juvenile literature. 2. Soldiers—United States—Juvenile literature. I. Title. II. Title: Soldados
del Ejército de Estados Unidos. III. Title: Soldiers of the U.S. Army. IV. Title: Soldiers of the United States Army.
UA25.S5717 2011
355.3'30973—dc22   2010041502

Editorial Credits
Gillia Olson, editor; Strictly Spanish, translation services; Renée T. Doyle, designer; Danielle Ceminsky,
    bilingual book designer; Laura Manthe, production specialist

Photo Credits
AP Images/Al Grillo, 15
Capstone Press/Gary Sundermeyer, 21
DoD photo by Senior Airman Steve Czyz, USAF, 17; Staff Sgt. Stacy L. Pearsall, USAF, 5
Photo Courtesy of Department of Defense, 19
Photo Courtesy of U.S. Army, 7, 9
Shutterstock/risteski goce, 22–23
U.S. Air Force photo by Staff Sgt Jason T. Bailey, 13
U.S. Army photo by Staff Sgt Adam Mancin, cover
U.S. Navy photo by MC2 Sandra M. Palumbo, 11

Artistic Effects
Shutterstock/ariadna de raadt (tank tire), 2–3, 24
Shutterstock/Tamer Yazici (camouflage), cover, 1

Note to Parents and Teachers

The Gente de las Fuerzas Armadas de EE.UU./People of the U.S. Armed Forces series
supports national science standards related to science, technology, and society. This book
describes and illustrates soldiers of the U.S. Army in both English and Spanish. The images
support early readers in understanding the text. The repetition of words and phrases helps early
readers learn new words. This book also introduces early readers to subject-specific vocabulary
words, which are defined in the Glossary section. Early readers may need assistance to read
some words and to use the Table of Contents, Glossary, Internet Sites, and Index sections of
the book.

Printed in the United States of America in North Mankato, Minnesota.
092010   005933CGS11

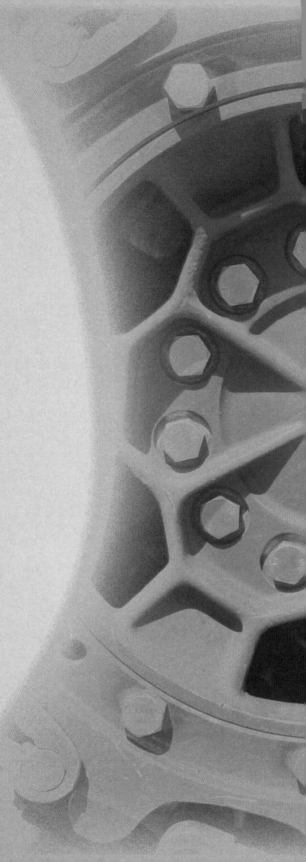

Table of Contents

Tabla de contenidos

Joining the Army

Men and women join the United States Army to defend the country. They protect the country on land.

Unirse al Ejército

Hombres y mujeres se unen al Ejército de Estados Unidos para defender al país. Ellos protegen al país en tierra.

Recruits have basic training for
10 weeks. They exercise, march,
and learn to read maps.
They learn about weapons.

Los reclutan reciben entrenamiento
básico durante 10 semanas.
Ellos hacen ejercicios, marchan
y aprenden a leer mapas. Ellos
aprenden acerca de las armas.

Job Training

After basic training, recruits are called soldiers. They learn new jobs. Some drive Strykers, which have armor to protect soldiers.

Entrenamiento para el trabajo

Después del entrenamiento básico, los reclutas son llamados soldados. Ellos aprenden nuevos trabajos. Algunos conducen Strykers, que tienen armamento para proteger a los soldados.

Infantry soldiers are trained
to fight on land. They find their
way with a Global Positioning
System (GPS).

Los soldados de infantería son
entrenados para pelear en tierra.
Ellos encuentran su camino con
un Sistema de Posicionamiento
Global (GPS).

Soldiers called engineers
design and build bridges
and roads.

Los soldados llamados ingenieros
diseñan y construyen puentes
y carreteras.

Living on Post

Many soldiers live in places called posts. Posts have homes, restaurants, and stores for soldiers and their families.

Vivir en un puesto

Muchos soldados viven en lugares llamados puestos. Los puestos tienen casas, restaurantes y tiendas para los soldados y sus familias.

Posts are in the United States
or other countries. A soldier
changes posts every three
to four years.

Hay puestos en Estados Unidos
y en otros países. Un soldado
cambia de puesto cada tres
a cuatro años.

Serving the Country

Most Army soldiers serve two to six years. Some soldiers serve 20 years or more. The Army is their career.

Servir al país

Muchos soldados del Ejército sirven de dos a seis años. Algunos soldados sirven durante 20 años o más. El Ejército es su carrera.

Soldiers who leave the Army are called civilians. Some find jobs. Others go to college.

Los soldados que dejan el Ejército se llaman civiles. Algunos buscan trabajo. Otros van a la universidad.

Glossary

basic training—the first training period for people who join the military

civilian—a person who is not in the military

infantry—a group of people in the military trained to fight on land

post—an area run by the military where people serving in the military live and military supplies are stored

recruit—a person who has just joined the military

Stryker—an armored vehicle

weapon—an object used to protect or attack

Internet Sites

FactHound offers a safe, fun way to find Internet sites related to this book. All of the sites on FactHound have been researched by our staff.

Here's all you do:

Visit *www.facthound.com*

Type in this code: 9781429661188

Super-cool stuff! Check out projects, games and lots more at **www.capstonekids.com**

Glosario

el arma—un objeto usado para proteger o atacar

civil—una persona que no está en las Fuerzas Armadas

el entrenamiento básico—el primer período de entrenamiento para las personas que se unen a las Fuerzas Armadas

la infantería—un grupo de personas en las Fuerzas Armadas entrenadas para pelear en tierra

el puesto—un área administrada por las Fuerzas Armadas donde vive la gente en servicio y donde se almacenan los suministros militares

el recluta—una persona que recién se unió a las Fuerzas Armadas

el Stryker—un vehículo con armamento

Sitios de Internet

FactHound brinda una forma segura y divertida de encontrar sitios de Internet relacionados con este libro. Todos los sitios en FactHound han sido investigados por nuestro personal.

Esto es todo lo que tienes que hacer:

Visita *www.facthound.com*

Ingresa este código: 9781429661188

Index

Índice